FINANCIAL FITNESS

Mastering Money Management and Wealth Creation

NANCY BARLOW

Copyright © 2024 by Nancy Barlow

All rights reserved. No part of this book may be reproduced, stored in a retrieval system, or transmitted, in any form or by any means, electronic, mechanical, photocopying, recording, or otherwise, without the prior written permission of the author, except in the case of brief quotations embodied in critical reviews and certain other noncommercial uses permitted by copyright law.

TABLE OF CONTENT

INTRODUCTION 5

CHAPTER 1: UNDERSTANDING YOUR FINANCIAL LANDSCAPE 8

- Assessing your current financial situation 10

- Identifying financial goals and priorities 14

- Exploring common financial challenges and obstacles 18

CHAPTER 2: BUILDING A SOLID FINANCIAL FOUNDATION 23

- Creating a realistic budget and spending plan 25

- Establishing an emergency fund 30

- Managing debt effectively 34

CHAPTER 3: INVESTING IN YOUR FUTURE 39

- Understanding risk and return 41

- Developing an investment strategy tailored to your goals and risk tolerance 47

CHAPTER 4: PLANNING FOR RETIREMENT 53

- Exploring different retirement accounts (401(k), IRA, Roth IRA, etc.) 55

- Calculating retirement savings goals 61

- Strategies for maximizing retirement savings and minimizing taxes 67

CHAPTER 5: ADVANCED WEALTH CREATION STRATEGIES 74

- Diversification and asset allocation 77

- Tax-efficient investing 86

- Estate planning and wealth preservation techniques 93

CONCLUSION 102

INTRODUCTION

Welcome to Financial Fitness: Mastering Money Management and Wealth Creation. In a world where financial literacy is paramount for success, this book serves as your comprehensive guide to navigating the intricate landscape of personal finance. Whether you're just starting your journey to financial independence or seeking to refine your existing strategies, this book offers a roadmap to achieving your goals.

Financial fitness is not merely about accumulating wealth; it's about developing a mindset and skill set that empower you to make informed decisions, cultivate healthy financial habits, and ultimately secure your financial future. In these pages, we delve into the fundamental principles of money management, explore strategies for building wealth, and provide practical advice for overcoming common financial challenges.

Drawing from years of experience and research, this book is designed to be accessible and actionable, offering insights that can be applied regardless of your current financial situation. From budgeting and saving to investing and retirement planning, each chapter is crafted to equip you with the knowledge and tools needed to take control of your financial destiny.

But financial fitness is not a destination; it's a journey. It requires dedication, discipline, and a willingness to learn and adapt. As you embark on this journey with us, remember that small steps taken today can lead to significant strides tomorrow. Whether your goal is to pay off debt, build a nest egg, or achieve financial freedom, this book will empower you to make meaningful progress towards your aspirations.

So, are you ready to embark on the path to financial fitness? Let's begin the journey together, as we master money management and unlock the keys to wealth creation.

CHAPTER 1: UNDERSTANDING YOUR FINANCIAL LANDSCAPE

Before embarking on any journey, it's essential to know where you stand and where you're headed. In the realm of personal finance, this journey begins with a thorough understanding of your financial landscape. Chapter 1 serves as your compass, guiding you through the process of assessing your current financial situation, identifying your goals, and navigating the terrain ahead.

In this chapter, we delve into the intricacies of your financial reality, examining factors such as income, expenses, assets, and liabilities. By taking stock of where you stand financially, you gain valuable insights into your strengths and weaknesses, enabling you to chart a course towards your desired destination.

Moreover, we explore the importance of setting clear financial goals and priorities. Whether your aspirations include buying a home, saving for your children's education, or achieving financial independence, defining your objectives provides the foundation for effective planning and decision-making.

Additionally, we shine a light on common financial challenges and obstacles that may impede your progress. From managing debt to coping with unexpected expenses, understanding these hurdles equips you with the knowledge and strategies needed to overcome them.

By the end of this chapter, you'll have gained a deeper understanding of your financial landscape, laying the groundwork for the journey ahead. Armed with this knowledge, you'll be better equipped to make informed decisions, seize opportunities, and ultimately, achieve financial success. So, let's embark on this exploration together, as we navigate the complexities of your financial terrain and pave the way for a brighter financial future.

- Assessing your current financial situation

Assessing your current financial situation is a critical first step in taking control of your finances and working towards your financial goals. This process involves thoroughly examining various aspects of your financial life to gain a clear understanding of where you stand financially. Here's a comprehensive discussion on how to assess your current financial situation:

1. **Gather Financial Information:** Begin by collecting all relevant financial documents, including bank statements, credit card statements, investment account statements, pay stubs, tax returns, and any other financial records. Having

these documents on hand will provide a comprehensive overview of your financial situation.

2. **Calculate Net Worth:** Calculate your net worth by subtracting your liabilities (debts) from your assets. Assets may include savings accounts, investments, real estate, vehicles, and valuable possessions. Liabilities encompass debts such as mortgages, student loans, credit card balances, and any other outstanding loans. Your net worth is a measure of your overall financial health and can help you track progress over time.

3. **Analyze Income and Expenses:** Review your income sources, including salary, wages, bonuses, rental income, and any other sources of income. Compare your total income to your monthly expenses to determine if you're living within your means. Categorize expenses into fixed (e.g., rent, mortgage, utilities) and variable (e.g., groceries, dining out, entertainment) to identify areas where you can potentially cut back or optimize spending.

4. **Assess Debt Levels:** Examine your outstanding debts, including balances, interest rates, and minimum monthly payments. Identify high-interest debts that may be prioritized for repayment, such as credit card debt. Consider the debt-to-income ratio, which measures your total monthly debt payments relative to your gross monthly income, as an indicator of your debt burden.

5. **Review Credit Report:** Obtain a copy of your credit report from each of the major credit bureaus (Equifax, Experian, TransUnion) and review it for accuracy. Check for any errors or inaccuracies that could negatively impact your credit score. Your credit report provides valuable insights into your borrowing and repayment history, which lenders use to evaluate your creditworthiness.

6. **Evaluate Savings and Emergency Fund:** Assess the adequacy of your savings and emergency fund. Aim to have enough savings to cover at least three to six months' worth of living expenses in case of unexpected emergencies, such as job loss, medical expenses, or major repairs.

7. Consider Financial Goals and Objectives:
Reflect on your short-term and long-term financial goals, such as buying a home, saving for retirement, paying for education, or traveling. Evaluate how your current financial situation aligns with these goals and identify any adjustments or strategies needed to achieve them.

8. **Seek Professional Advice:** If you're unsure about your financial situation or need guidance on specific financial matters, consider consulting with a financial advisor or planner. A professional can offer personalized advice and strategies tailored to your circumstances and goals.

By thoroughly assessing your current financial situation, you gain valuable insights into your financial strengths, weaknesses, and areas for improvement. This knowledge forms the foundation for creating a comprehensive financial plan and making informed decisions to secure your financial future. Remember that financial circumstances may change over time, so it's essential to periodically reassess your financial situation and adjust your strategies accordingly.

- Identifying financial goals and priorities

Identifying financial goals and priorities is a crucial step in the process of managing your finances effectively and achieving financial success. These goals serve as the guiding principles that inform your financial decisions and actions. Here's a comprehensive discussion on how to identify financial goals and priorities:

1. **Reflect on Personal Values and Aspirations:** Start by reflecting on your personal values, aspirations, and dreams. What do you envision for your future? What are your priorities in life? Understanding what truly matters to you will help you identify financial goals that align with your values and aspirations.

2. **Distinguish Between Short-Term and Long-Term Goals:** Categorize your financial goals into

short-term, medium-term, and long-term objectives. Short-term goals may include building an emergency fund, paying off credit card debt, or taking a vacation. Medium-term goals could involve saving for a down payment on a home, funding your children's education, or purchasing a car. Long-term goals typically revolve around retirement planning, such as building a sizable retirement nest egg or achieving financial independence.

3. **Make Goals Specific, Measurable, Achievable, Relevant, and Time-Bound (SMART):** Ensure that your financial goals are SMART:

- **Specific:** Clearly define what you want to accomplish.

- **Measurable:** Establish criteria for measuring progress and success.

- **Achievable:** Set goals that are realistic and attainable within your current financial circumstances.

- **Relevant:** Align your goals with your values, priorities, and life stage.

- **Time-Bound:** Set deadlines or timeframes for achieving each goal to create a sense of urgency and accountability.

4. **Prioritize Goals:** Determine the relative importance of each financial goal based on your values, timeline, and financial capacity. Some goals may take precedence over others, requiring more immediate attention and resources. For example, building an emergency fund may take priority over discretionary spending on non-essential items.

5. **Quantify Goals and Establish Targets:** Quantify your financial goals by attaching specific dollar amounts or percentages to each objective. Whether it's saving a certain amount for retirement, paying off a specific debt balance, or accumulating a down payment for a home, having clear targets makes it easier to track progress and stay motivated.

6. **Consider Trade-Offs and Sacrifices:** Recognize that achieving financial goals often requires trade-offs and sacrifices. Evaluate the impact of your spending habits and lifestyle choices on your ability

to reach your goals. Determine what expenses can be reduced or eliminated to allocate more resources towards your top priorities.

7. **Review and Revise Goals Regularly:** Periodically review and reassess your financial goals to ensure they remain relevant and aligned with your evolving needs and circumstances. Life changes, such as marriage, career transitions, or unexpected events, may necessitate adjustments to your goals and priorities.

8. **Seek Accountability and Support:** Share your financial goals with trusted friends, family members, or a financial advisor who can provide support, encouragement, and accountability. Having someone to hold you accountable can help you stay focused and committed to achieving your goals.

By identifying clear financial goals and priorities, you set yourself on a path towards financial success and fulfillment. These goals serve as the roadmap that guides your financial decisions, motivates your actions, and ultimately leads to a brighter financial future. Remember that achieving financial goals is a journey that requires dedication, perseverance, and strategic planning.

- Exploring common financial challenges and obstacles

Exploring common financial challenges and obstacles is essential for gaining insight into the hurdles that individuals often encounter on their financial journeys. By understanding these challenges, you can develop strategies to overcome them and achieve greater financial stability. Here's a comprehensive discussion of some of the most prevalent financial challenges and obstacles:

1. **Debt Management:** Debt is a pervasive issue for many individuals, whether it's student loans, credit card debt, mortgages, or personal loans. High levels of debt can strain finances, hinder savings efforts, and limit opportunities for wealth accumulation.

Effective debt management strategies, such as budgeting, debt consolidation, and prioritizing high-interest debt repayment, are essential for regaining control of your finances.

2. **Insufficient Savings:** Many people struggle with inadequate savings, whether it's an emergency fund, retirement savings, or other financial goals. Without a sufficient safety net, unexpected expenses or life events can lead to financial hardship and stress. Building a habit of regular saving, automating contributions to savings accounts, and setting specific savings goals are crucial steps towards establishing a solid financial foundation.

3. **Lack of Financial Literacy:** A lack of financial literacy and understanding of basic financial concepts can pose significant challenges for individuals trying to manage their finances effectively. Without the necessary knowledge and skills, individuals may make uninformed decisions, fall victim to financial scams, or fail to optimize their financial resources. Investing in financial education through workshops, courses, or self-study

can empower individuals to make better financial decisions and navigate complex financial matters confidently.

4. **Unplanned Expenses and Emergencies:** Unexpected expenses, such as medical bills, car repairs, or home maintenance, can derail financial plans and strain budgets. Without adequate preparation, individuals may resort to high-interest borrowing or deplete savings to cover these expenses, exacerbating financial stress. Establishing an emergency fund and regularly contributing to it can provide a financial safety net to weather unforeseen challenges.

5. **Inadequate Retirement Planning:** Many individuals underestimate the importance of retirement planning and fail to adequately prepare for their golden years. With increasing life expectancy and uncertainty surrounding social security benefits, it's essential to save diligently for retirement and develop a comprehensive retirement plan. Starting early, maximizing contributions to retirement accounts, and diversifying investments

are key strategies for ensuring a comfortable retirement lifestyle.

6. **Job Loss or Income Reduction:** Job loss, income reduction, or other employment-related setbacks can have devastating financial consequences, leading to financial instability and hardship. It's crucial to have contingency plans in place, such as an emergency fund, unemployment insurance, or alternative income streams, to mitigate the impact of unexpected job loss or income disruptions.

7. **Healthcare Costs and Insurance:** Rising healthcare costs and inadequate insurance coverage can pose significant financial challenges for individuals and families. Medical emergencies or chronic health conditions can lead to substantial out-of-pocket expenses, even for those with health insurance. Understanding health insurance options, maximizing coverage, and budgeting for healthcare expenses are essential for managing this financial risk.

8. Behavioral Biases and Emotional Decision-Making: Behavioral biases, such as overconfidence, loss aversion, and herd mentality, can influence financial decision-making and lead to suboptimal outcomes. Emotional responses to market volatility or financial setbacks may prompt individuals to make impulsive decisions that undermine long-term financial goals. Developing self-awareness, practicing mindfulness, and seeking objective financial advice can help individuals overcome these biases and make more rational financial decisions.

By exploring these common financial challenges and obstacles, individuals can proactively address them and implement strategies to improve their financial well-being. It's important to recognize that financial success is not about avoiding challenges altogether but rather about building resilience and adaptability to navigate challenges effectively on the path towards achieving financial goals.

CHAPTER 2: BUILDING A SOLID FINANCIAL FOUNDATION

Welcome to Chapter 2: Building a Solid Financial Foundation. Just as a sturdy building requires a strong foundation to withstand the test of time, your financial well-being hinges on the strength of your financial foundation. In this chapter, we delve into the essential elements that form the bedrock of your financial stability and success.

Building a solid financial foundation is not just about amassing wealth; it's about establishing sound financial habits, managing resources wisely, and protecting yourself against unexpected setbacks. It's the cornerstone upon which you can build a future of financial security and independence.

Throughout this chapter, we will explore key strategies and principles for laying the groundwork of your financial foundation:

1. **Creating a Realistic Budget and Spending Plan:** A budget serves as your financial roadmap, guiding your spending decisions and helping you allocate resources effectively. We'll discuss the importance of budgeting, how to create a personalized budget that reflects your priorities and goals, and practical tips for sticking to your budget.

2. **Establishing an Emergency Fund:** Life is full of uncertainties, and unexpected expenses can arise when you least expect them. An emergency fund provides a financial safety net to weather unforeseen challenges without derailing your financial progress. We'll explore why an emergency fund is essential, how much you should save, and where to keep your emergency fund for easy access.

3. **Managing Debt Effectively:** Debt can be a double-edged sword, providing growth opportunities but also posing risks to your financial stability. We'll discuss strategies for managing debt effectively, including prioritizing debt repayment, consolidating high-interest debt, and avoiding common debt traps.

By focusing on these fundamental aspects of financial management, you'll lay a solid foundation that empowers you to achieve your financial goals, weather financial storms, and build a brighter financial future. Whether you're just starting your journey to financial independence or seeking to enhance your financial health, the principles outlined in this chapter will serve as guiding principles to help you navigate the complexities of personal finance.

So, let's roll up our sleeves and start building a solid financial foundation that will support your dreams and aspirations for years to come.

- Creating a realistic budget and spending plan

Creating a realistic budget and spending plan is a fundamental aspect of personal finance that empowers individuals to take control of their financial lives, achieve their goals, and build a solid financial foundation. A budget serves as a roadmap for managing income and expenses, allowing individuals to allocate resources effectively and make informed financial decisions. Here's a comprehensive discussion on creating a realistic budget and spending plan:

1. **Assess Income:** Begin by determining your total monthly income from all sources, including salaries, wages, bonuses, commissions, rental income, investment dividends, and any other sources of income. It's essential to have an accurate understanding of your income to create a realistic budget.

2. **Track Expenses:** Track your expenses over a set period, such as a month, to understand where your money is going. Categorize expenses into fixed expenses (e.g., rent/mortgage, utilities, insurance) and variable expenses (e.g., groceries, dining out, entertainment). Use bank statements, credit card statements, receipts, and expense-tracking apps to capture all expenditures accurately.

3. Identify Financial Goals and Priorities: Determine your short-term and long-term financial goals, such as saving for emergencies, paying off debt, saving for retirement, buying a home, or funding education. Prioritize your goals based on their importance and urgency, allocating resources accordingly in your budget.

4. Set Spending Limits: Based on your income and financial goals, establish spending limits for each expense category in your budget. Be realistic and flexible when setting limits, considering your lifestyle, needs, and priorities. Allocate a portion of your income towards essential expenses, savings, debt repayment, and discretionary spending.

5. Differentiate Needs vs. Wants: Differentiate between essential needs and discretionary wants when budgeting. Essential needs are necessities required for survival and basic living, such as food, shelter, transportation, and healthcare. Discretionary wants are non-essential expenses for luxury items or entertainment. Prioritize spending on needs while allocating discretionary funds based on your financial goals and priorities.

6. **Account for Irregular Expenses and Seasonal Variations:** Anticipate irregular expenses, such as annual insurance premiums, vehicle maintenance, holiday expenses, or quarterly taxes, by budgeting for them monthly. Set aside funds in separate sinking funds or savings accounts to cover these irregular expenses when they arise, preventing financial strain.

7. **Review and Adjust Regularly:** Regularly review and adjust your budget to reflect changes in income, expenses, financial goals, and life circumstances. As your financial situation evolves, you may need to reallocate resources, revise spending priorities, or adjust spending limits accordingly. Flexibility and adaptability are key to maintaining a realistic budget over time.

8. **Use Budgeting Tools and Apps:** Leverage budgeting tools, spreadsheets, or budgeting apps to streamline the budgeting process and track expenses

efficiently. Many apps offer features such as expense categorization, spending alerts, goal tracking, and budgeting insights to help you stay organized and accountable.

9. **Monitor Progress and Stay Disciplined:** Monitor your progress towards financial goals and track actual spending against budgeted amounts regularly. Stay disciplined and committed to sticking to your budget, avoiding impulsive purchases or overspending in discretionary categories. Celebrate milestones and achievements along the way to stay motivated.

By creating a realistic budget and spending plan, individuals can gain control over their finances, prioritize their goals, and make intentional choices that align with their values and aspirations. A well-crafted budget serves as a powerful tool for achieving financial stability, reducing financial stress, and ultimately realizing financial freedom.

- Establishing an emergency fund

Establishing an emergency fund is a crucial component of financial planning that provides a financial safety net to protect against unexpected expenses, job loss, medical emergencies, or other unforeseen events. An emergency fund serves as a buffer, allowing individuals to cover essential expenses without relying on high-interest borrowing or depleting long-term savings. Here's a comprehensive discussion on establishing an emergency fund:

1. **Understanding the Purpose:** The primary purpose of an emergency fund is to provide financial security and peace of mind during times of crisis or unexpected hardship. It serves as a reserve of liquid funds that can be accessed quickly and easily when needed, without resorting to debt or liquidating assets.

2. **Determining the Target Amount:** The ideal size of an emergency fund varies depending on individual circumstances, such as income level, family size, lifestyle, and financial obligations. Financial experts generally recommend saving enough to cover three to six months' worth of living expenses. However, individuals with unstable income, high financial obligations, or greater risk factors may need to aim for a larger emergency fund.

3. **Calculating Living Expenses:** Calculate your monthly living expenses, including housing costs, utilities, groceries, transportation, insurance premiums, loan payments, and other essential expenses. Multiply your average monthly expenses by the recommended number of months (e.g., three to six) to determine your target emergency fund amount.

4. **Starting Small and Building Over Time:** If saving a large emergency fund seems daunting, start small and gradually build your reserves over time. Set achievable savings goals and contribute

regularly to your emergency fund, even if it's initially a modest amount. Consistency and discipline are key to growing your emergency fund steadily.

5. **Automating Contributions:** Make saving for emergencies a priority by automating contributions to your emergency fund. Set up automatic transfers from your paycheck or checking account to a dedicated savings account earmarked for emergencies. Treating emergency savings as a non-negotiable expense ensures that you consistently allocate funds towards this critical goal.

6. **Choosing the Right Account:** Store your emergency fund in a highly liquid, easily accessible account, such as a high-yield savings account, money market account, or a dedicated emergency savings account. Avoid tying up funds in investments or accounts with penalties for early withdrawal, as you may need to access the funds quickly in an emergency.

7. **Resisting Temptation:** Resist the temptation to dip into your emergency fund for non-urgent expenses or discretionary purchases. Keep the funds separate from your everyday spending accounts and avoid using them for anything other than genuine emergencies. Establishing clear criteria for what constitutes an emergency can help prevent frivolous withdrawals.

8. **Replenishing and Maintaining:** Regularly review and replenish your emergency fund as needed, especially after tapping into it for emergencies. Life changes, such as job loss, medical expenses, or major repairs, may deplete your emergency fund, necessitating replenishment. Aim to maintain your emergency fund at the target level to ensure ongoing financial security.

9. **Adjusting for Life Changes:** Periodically reassess your emergency fund needs in light of life changes, such as marriage, childbirth, career transitions, or changes in living expenses. Adjust your savings goals and emergency fund

contributions accordingly to reflect changes in your financial situation and needs.

Establishing an emergency fund is an essential step towards achieving financial resilience and stability. By prioritizing emergency savings and building a sufficient financial cushion, individuals can navigate unexpected challenges with confidence, protect their financial well-being, and pursue their long-term financial goals without undue financial stress.

- Managing debt effectively

Managing debt effectively is a critical aspect of personal finance that can significantly impact your financial health and well-being. Debt, when used responsibly, can be a useful tool for achieving financial goals such as homeownership, education, or starting a business. However, excessive debt or mismanagement of debt can lead to financial stress, high-interest payments, and hindered progress towards financial goals. Here's a comprehensive discussion on managing debt effectively:

1. **Assess Your Debt:** Begin by assessing your current debt situation. Compile a list of all outstanding debts, including credit card balances, student loans, auto loans, personal loans, mortgages, and any other liabilities. Note the total amount owed, interest rates, minimum monthly payments, and terms of each debt.

2. **Prioritize High-Interest Debt:** Prioritize paying off high-interest debt first, such as credit card debt or payday loans. These types of debt typically carry the highest interest rates, resulting in substantial interest charges and prolonged repayment periods. By focusing on high-interest debt, you can minimize interest expenses and accelerate debt payoff.

3. **Create a Debt Repayment Plan:** Develop a structured debt repayment plan that outlines how you will tackle each debt systematically. Consider using the debt snowball or debt avalanche method

to prioritize debts based on either the balance (snowball) or interest rate (avalanche). Allocate extra funds towards debt repayment by trimming discretionary expenses, increasing income, or reallocating savings.

4. **Negotiate Lower Interest Rates or Payment Terms:** Contact creditors or lenders to negotiate lower interest rates, extended payment terms, or alternative repayment arrangements, such as debt consolidation or refinancing. Lowering interest rates can reduce the overall cost of debt and make repayment more manageable, especially for high-interest loans or credit card balances.

5. **Consolidate Debt Wisely:** Explore debt consolidation options, such as balance transfer credit cards, personal loans, or home equity loans, to consolidate multiple debts into a single, more manageable payment. Consolidation can simplify repayment, lower interest rates, and streamline debt management, but it's essential to weigh the pros and cons and ensure that you're not accruing additional debt.

6. **Avoid Taking on New Debt:** Minimize the temptation to take on new debt while repaying existing obligations. Practice discipline and restraint when it comes to borrowing for non-essential purchases or discretionary expenses. Consider implementing a cash-only or debit card policy for everyday spending to avoid accumulating additional debt.

7. **Build an Emergency Fund:** Establishing an emergency fund is essential for managing debt effectively. Having a financial safety net in place can help cover unexpected expenses or financial setbacks without resorting to high-interest borrowing or increasing debt levels. Aim to save three to six months' worth of living expenses in an easily accessible account dedicated to emergencies.

8. **Seek Professional Advice if Needed:** If you're struggling to manage debt or feeling overwhelmed by your financial situation, consider seeking professional advice from a certified credit counselor, financial planner, or debt relief specialist. These professionals can provide

personalized guidance, debt management strategies, and resources to help you regain control of your finances.

9. **Stay Committed and Persistent:** Managing debt effectively requires commitment, discipline, and persistence over time. Stay focused on your debt repayment goals, celebrate small victories along the way, and remain patient as you progress towards becoming debt-free. Consistency and perseverance are key to achieving long-term financial freedom.

By implementing these strategies and adopting responsible borrowing habits, you can effectively manage debt, reduce financial stress, and work towards achieving your financial goals. Remember that managing debt is a journey, and progress may take time, but with determination and proactive financial management, you can regain control of your finances and pave the way to a brighter financial future.

CHAPTER 3: INVESTING IN YOUR FUTURE

Welcome to Chapter 3: Investing in Your Future. In this chapter, we embark on a journey into the world of investing—a realm where strategic decisions today can shape your financial future tomorrow. Investing is not merely about allocating money; it's about planting seeds of wealth creation, nurturing them over time, and reaping the rewards of disciplined patience and prudent decision-making.

Investing is a powerful tool for building wealth, achieving financial goals, and securing your long-term financial well-being. Whether you're saving for retirement, funding your children's education, or pursuing financial independence, investing offers opportunities for growth, diversification, and wealth accumulation.

Throughout this chapter, we'll explore the fundamental principles of investing, from understanding different asset classes to developing a personalized investment strategy tailored to your goals, risk tolerance, and time horizon. We'll delve into the nuances of risk and return, explore various investment options, and discuss practical strategies for building and managing an investment portfolio.

But investing is not without its challenges and complexities. Market volatility, economic uncertainty, and behavioral biases can impact investment decisions and outcomes. Therefore, we'll also discuss strategies for mitigating risks, managing emotions, and staying focused on long-term goals amidst market fluctuations.

Whether you're a novice investor just starting your journey or a seasoned veteran seeking to refine your approach, this chapter will equip you with the knowledge, tools, and confidence needed to navigate the investment landscape effectively. By harnessing the power of investing, you'll position yourself to capitalize on opportunities, grow your wealth, and secure a brighter financial future for yourself and your loved ones.

So, join us as we embark on this exploration of investing in your future. Let's unlock the potential of the financial markets, harness the power of compounding, and set sail towards a future of financial abundance and prosperity.

- Introduction to various investment options (stocks, bonds, mutual funds, real estate, etc.)

- Understanding risk and return

Understanding risk and return is fundamental to making informed investment decisions and building a successful investment portfolio. Risk and return are two sides of the same coin in investing, with higher potential returns typically associated with higher levels of risk. Here's a comprehensive discussion on understanding risk and return in investing:

1. **Definition of Risk and Return:**

   - **Risk:** Risk refers to the uncertainty or variability of investment returns. It encompasses the possibility of losing some or all of the invested capital, as well as the potential for volatility in investment performance. Different types of risk include market risk, credit risk, liquidity risk, inflation risk, and geopolitical risk.

   - **Return:** Return represents the gain or loss on an investment over a specified period, usually expressed as a percentage of the initial investment. It reflects the amount of profit or loss generated from an investment, including capital appreciation, dividends, interest, or other income.

2. **Risk-Return Tradeoff:**

   - The risk-return tradeoff is a fundamental concept in investing that suggests higher potential returns are generally associated with higher levels of risk, and vice versa. Investors must balance their risk tolerance with their return objectives when making investment decisions.

- Risk-averse investors, who prioritize capital preservation and are unwilling to accept significant fluctuations in value, may opt for lower-risk investments with lower expected returns, such as bonds or cash equivalents.

- Risk-tolerant investors, who are comfortable with volatility and seek higher potential returns, may allocate a greater portion of their portfolio to higher-risk investments, such as stocks or alternative assets.

3. **Types of Risk:**

- **Market Risk:** Market risk, also known as systematic risk, refers to the risk of fluctuations in the overall market that affect all investments. Factors such as economic conditions, interest rates, geopolitical events, and market sentiment can impact market risk.

- **Specific Risk:** Specific risk, also known as unsystematic risk, is the risk specific to an individual investment or asset class. It can be mitigated through diversification, which involves spreading investments across multiple assets to reduce exposure to any single source of risk.

- **Inflation Risk:** Inflation risk arises from the erosion of purchasing power over time due to rising inflation rates. Investments that fail to outpace inflation may result in a loss of real value over time.

- **Credit Risk:** Credit risk, or default risk, refers to the risk of an issuer failing to meet its debt obligations, resulting in potential loss of principal or interest payments for bondholders.

- **Liquidity Risk:** Liquidity risk is the risk associated with the inability to buy or sell an investment quickly and at a fair price. Investments with lower liquidity may be subject to wider bid-ask spreads and price volatility.

4. **Measuring Risk and Return:**

   - Various metrics and ratios are used to measure risk and return, including standard deviation, beta, Sharpe ratio, and alpha. These tools provide insights into the volatility, correlation, risk-adjusted returns, and performance relative to a benchmark or index.

- Investors should consider both historical performance and prospects when evaluating risk and return. Past performance is not indicative of future results, and investors should conduct thorough due diligence and analysis before making investment decisions.

5. **Diversification and Risk Management:**

- Diversification is a strategy that involves spreading investments across different asset classes, industries, sectors, and geographic regions to reduce risk and enhance portfolio stability. By diversifying, investors can potentially mitigate the impact of individual assets or market fluctuations on their overall portfolio.

- Asset allocation, or the strategic distribution of assets across different investment categories, is another key aspect of risk management. By allocating assets based on risk tolerance, investment objectives, and time horizon, investors can tailor their portfolios to achieve a balance between risk and return.

6. Investment Horizon and Risk:

- The investment horizon, or the length of time an investor expects to hold an investment, influences risk tolerance and investment decisions. Longer investment horizons generally allow investors to withstand short-term fluctuations and pursue higher-risk, higher-return investments, such as equities, with the potential for long-term growth.

- Shorter investment horizons may necessitate a more conservative approach, focusing on preserving capital and minimizing downside risk.

7. Risk Management Strategies:

- Risk management strategies aim to identify, assess, and mitigate potential risks to investment portfolios. These strategies may include asset allocation, diversification, hedging, stop-loss orders, and portfolio rebalancing.

- Regular monitoring and review of portfolio performance, economic indicators, and market conditions are essential for identifying emerging risks and adjusting investment strategies accordingly.

Understanding the relationship between risk and return is essential for making informed investment decisions and constructing a well-diversified portfolio that aligns with your financial goals, risk tolerance, and investment horizon. By carefully evaluating risk factors, implementing risk management strategies, and diversifying across asset classes, investors can optimize their risk-return profiles and enhance the likelihood of achieving long-term investment success.

- Developing an investment strategy tailored to your goals and risk tolerance

Developing an investment strategy tailored to your goals and risk tolerance is essential for achieving long-term financial success while managing investment risk effectively. An investment strategy outlines a structured approach to allocating assets, selecting investments, and managing portfolios in line with your financial objectives, time horizon, and risk tolerance. Here's a comprehensive discussion on developing an investment strategy tailored to your goals and risk tolerance:

1. **Identify Financial Goals:** Begin by defining your financial goals and objectives. These goals may include saving for retirement, funding education expenses, purchasing a home, building wealth, or achieving financial independence. Each goal should be specific, measurable, achievable, relevant, and time-bound (SMART), providing a clear target for your investment strategy.

2. **Assess Risk Tolerance:** Determine your risk tolerance, or your willingness and ability to accept investment risk. Risk tolerance is influenced by factors such as investment experience, time horizon, financial capacity, income stability, and emotional temperament. Consider using risk tolerance

questionnaires or assessments offered by financial institutions or advisors to gauge your risk tolerance accurately.

3. **Understand Investment Options:** Familiarize yourself with different asset classes, investment products, and strategies available in the financial markets. Common asset classes include stocks, bonds, cash equivalents, real estate, commodities, and alternative investments. Each asset class has unique risk-return characteristics, correlations, and suitability for specific investment goals and risk profiles.

4. **Align Investments with Goals and Risk Tolerance:** Match your investment choices with your financial goals and risk tolerance. Conservative investors with lower risk tolerance may prefer a portfolio weighted towards fixed-income investments, such as bonds or cash equivalents, to prioritize capital preservation and income generation. Aggressive investors with higher risk tolerance may favor an equity-heavy portfolio to pursue higher growth potential.

5. **Diversify Portfolio:** Diversification is a key principle of risk management and involves spreading investments across multiple asset classes, sectors, industries, and geographic regions. Diversification helps reduce portfolio volatility, minimize the impact of individual asset performance, and enhance risk-adjusted returns. Consider your risk tolerance, investment goals, and time horizon when determining the appropriate asset allocation for your portfolio.

6. **Asset Allocation:** Determine the optimal asset allocation for your investment portfolio based on your goals, risk tolerance, and investment horizon. Asset allocation refers to the strategic distribution of assets across different investment categories, such as stocks, bonds, and cash equivalents. Common asset allocation strategies include aggressive, moderate, conservative, and balanced portfolios, each tailored to different risk profiles and investment objectives.

7. **Regular Review and Rebalancing:** Regularly review your investment portfolio to ensure

alignment with your goals, risk tolerance, and market conditions. Rebalance your portfolio periodically to maintain target asset allocations and adjust for changes in market values or investment performance. Rebalancing involves buying or selling assets to restore the desired asset mix, minimizing portfolio drift and optimizing risk-return characteristics.

8. **Consider Tax Efficiency:** Incorporate tax-efficient investment strategies to minimize the impact of taxes on investment returns. Utilize tax-advantaged accounts, such as IRAs, 401(k)s, and HSAs, to defer or avoid taxes on investment gains, dividends, and interest income. Implement tax-loss harvesting, asset location strategies, and capital gains management techniques to optimize after-tax returns.

9. **Stay Informed and Seek Professional Advice:** Stay informed about market developments, economic trends, and investment opportunities relevant to your investment strategy. Regularly educate yourself on investment principles,

strategies, and best practices. Consider seeking professional advice from certified financial planners, investment advisors, or wealth managers to develop and implement a tailored investment strategy that aligns with your goals and risk tolerance.

By developing an investment strategy tailored to your goals and risk tolerance, you can construct a diversified portfolio that balances risk and return, maximizes the likelihood of achieving your financial objectives, and provides a solid foundation for long-term wealth accumulation. Remember that investing is a dynamic and ongoing process, requiring periodic review, adjustments, and adherence to your established investment strategy.

CHAPTER 4: PLANNING FOR RETIREMENT

Welcome to Chapter 4: Planning for Retirement. Retirement is a significant milestone in life—a time when you transition from the workforce to a new chapter of leisure, fulfillment, and financial independence. However, achieving a secure and comfortable retirement requires careful planning, diligent saving, and informed decision-making.

In this chapter, we explore the essential aspects of retirement planning, from setting retirement goals to estimating retirement expenses, creating a retirement income strategy, and navigating retirement investment options. Whether you're just beginning your career, approaching retirement age, or already retired, this chapter will provide valuable insights and practical strategies to help you build a robust retirement plan that aligns with your aspirations and financial circumstances.

Retirement planning is not a one-size-fits-all endeavor—it's a personalized journey tailored to your unique goals, lifestyle preferences, risk tolerance, and time horizon. By taking proactive steps to plan for retirement now, you can lay the groundwork for a financially secure and fulfilling retirement lifestyle in the future.

Throughout this chapter, we'll address key questions and considerations, such as:

- How much do I need to save for retirement?

- What are my retirement income sources, including Social Security, pensions, and retirement accounts?

- How can I maximize retirement savings through employer-sponsored plans like 401(k)s and IRAs?

- What investment strategies are appropriate for retirement portfolios, considering risk tolerance and time horizon?

- How do I navigate healthcare costs, long-term care, and estate planning in retirement?

Whether retirement is decades away or just around the corner, the principles and strategies outlined in this chapter will empower you to take control of your financial future and embark on a journey towards a rewarding and fulfilling retirement. So, let's dive into the world of retirement planning and chart a course towards a secure and prosperous retirement lifestyle.

- Exploring different retirement accounts (401(k), IRA, Roth IRA, etc.)

Exploring different retirement accounts is essential for effective retirement planning, as these accounts offer tax advantages, investment options, and flexibility in saving for retirement. Understanding the features, benefits, and limitations of various retirement accounts can help individuals make informed decisions about where to allocate their retirement savings. Here's a comprehensive discussion of some of the most common retirement accounts:

1. 401(k) Plans:

- A 401(k) plan is an employer-sponsored retirement savings account offered by many private companies and some non-profit organizations.

- Contributions to a traditional 401(k) plan are made on a pre-tax basis, meaning they are deducted from your paycheck before taxes are withheld. This reduces your taxable income for the year and allows contributions to grow tax-deferred until withdrawal.

- Many employers offer matching contributions, where they match a portion of employee contributions up to a certain percentage of salary. This matching contribution is essentially free money and can significantly boost retirement savings.

- Withdrawals from traditional 401(k) accounts are taxed as ordinary income in retirement.

- Some employers offer Roth 401(k) options, where contributions are made after tax but withdrawals in retirement are tax-free.

2. **Individual Retirement Accounts (IRAs):**

- IRAs are personal retirement savings accounts that individuals can open independently of their employer.

- Traditional IRAs allow tax-deductible contributions, similar to traditional 401(k) plans, with earnings growing tax-deferred until withdrawal. Contributions are subject to annual contribution limits.

- Roth IRAs accept after-tax contributions, but qualified withdrawals in retirement, including earnings, are tax-free. Roth IRAs also offer tax-free withdrawals of contributions at any time.

- IRAs offer a wide range of investment options, including stocks, bonds, mutual funds, exchange-traded funds (ETFs), and more.

- Contribution limits for IRAs are lower than those for 401(k) plans, and eligibility may be subject to income limitations and participation in employer-sponsored plans.

3. Rollover IRAs:

- Rollover IRAs are traditional IRAs used to consolidate funds from employer-sponsored retirement plans, such as 401(k) plans, when changing jobs or retiring.

- Direct rollovers from qualified plans to rollover IRAs allow individuals to maintain the tax-deferred status of retirement savings without incurring taxes or penalties.

- Rollover IRAs offer greater control and flexibility over investment choices compared to employer-sponsored plans, which may have limited investment options.

4. SEP IRAs and SIMPLE IRAs:

- SEP (Simplified Employee Pension) IRAs and SIMPLE (Savings Incentive Match Plan for Employees) IRAs are retirement plans designed for self-employed individuals and small businesses.

- SEP IRAs allow employers to contribute a percentage of employees' salaries to individual retirement accounts. Contributions are tax-deductible for employers and tax-deferred for employees.

- SIMPLE IRAs are similar to 401(k) plans for small businesses, allowing both employer and employee contributions. Contributions are tax-deductible for employers and tax-deferred for employees.

5. Solo 401(k) Plans:

- Solo 401(k) plans, also known as individual 401(k) plans or self-employed 401(k) plans, are retirement savings vehicles for self-employed individuals or small business owners with no employees other than a spouse.

- Solo 401(k) plans offer higher contribution limits than traditional IRAs or SEP IRAs, allowing individuals to contribute as both employer and employee.

- Like traditional 401(k) plans, contributions to solo 401(k) plans are made on a pre-tax basis, with earnings growing tax-deferred until withdrawal.

6. **457(b) Plans and 403(b) Plans:**

- 457(b) plans are employer-sponsored retirement plans available to employees of state and local governments, as well as some non-profit organizations.

- 403(b) plans are similar to 401(k) plans but are offered by certain tax-exempt organizations, such as schools, hospitals, and religious organizations.

- Contributions to 457(b) and 403(b) plans are made on a pre-tax basis, with tax-deferred growth until withdrawal. Roth options may also be available in some plans.

Each type of retirement account has its own set of features, eligibility requirements, contribution limits, and tax implications. Individuals should carefully consider their financial goals, risk tolerance, and tax situation when selecting retirement accounts and allocating contributions. Consulting with a financial advisor or tax professional can provide personalized guidance and help individuals make informed decisions based on their unique circumstances. By exploring different retirement accounts and maximizing contributions to tax-advantaged accounts, individuals can take significant steps towards building a secure and prosperous retirement future.

- Calculating retirement savings goals

Calculating retirement savings goals is a critical step in retirement planning, as it helps individuals determine how much they need to save to maintain their desired lifestyle in retirement. Retirement savings goals are influenced by various factors, including current age, desired retirement age, life expectancy, expected retirement expenses, inflation, investment returns, and retirement income sources. Here's a comprehensive discussion on calculating retirement savings goals:

1. **Estimate Retirement Expenses:**

   - Begin by estimating your retirement expenses, including both essential and discretionary expenses. Essential expenses may include housing, utilities, food, healthcare, transportation, insurance premiums, and taxes. Discretionary expenses may include travel, hobbies, entertainment, and other lifestyle choices.

   - Consider potential changes in expenses during retirement, such as healthcare costs, long-term care needs, inflation, and adjustments to lifestyle preferences.

   - Use current expenses as a starting point and adjust for changes in spending patterns, needs, and circumstances expected in retirement.

2. Determine Retirement Income Needs:

- Calculate the income needed to cover retirement expenses after accounting for other sources of retirement income, such as Social Security benefits, pensions, annuities, rental income, part-time work, or other passive income streams.

- Estimate Social Security benefits using online calculators provided by the Social Security Administration or financial planning tools. Consider factors such as full retirement age, delayed retirement credits, and spousal benefits.

- Evaluate other potential income sources, such as pensions from current or former employers, annuity payments, rental income from real estate investments, or royalties from intellectual property.

3. Assess Longevity and Life Expectancy:

- Consider your life expectancy and potential longevity in retirement when calculating retirement savings goals. Use life expectancy calculators or actuarial tables to estimate how long you may live in retirement.

- Plan for a retirement period that may span several decades, especially considering advancements in healthcare and increased life expectancies.

4. Factor in Inflation and Future Expenses:

- Account for inflation when estimating future expenses and income needs in retirement. Inflation erodes purchasing power over time, meaning that the same amount of money will buy less in the future.

- Adjust retirement savings goals and income projections to account for the impact of inflation on living expenses, healthcare costs, and other retirement expenditures.

5. Calculate Retirement Savings Gap:

- Determine the shortfall or "retirement savings gap" between projected retirement expenses and expected retirement income sources. The retirement savings gap represents the amount that needs to be funded through personal savings and investment accounts to maintain the desired lifestyle in retirement.

- Subtract expected retirement income, including Social Security benefits, pensions, and other income sources, from estimated retirement expenses to determine the retirement savings gap.

6. Use Retirement Calculators and Tools:

- Utilize retirement planning calculators, online tools, or financial planning software to perform detailed retirement savings projections. These tools can help estimate retirement savings goals, analyze various scenarios, and identify strategies to bridge the retirement savings gap.

- Input key variables such as current age, desired retirement age, life expectancy, retirement expenses, expected investment returns, inflation rates, and other relevant factors to generate personalized retirement savings projections.

7. **Adjust Savings Strategies and Assumptions:**

   - Review and adjust retirement savings goals periodically based on changes in personal circumstances, financial goals, economic conditions, and market trends.

   - Consider modifying savings strategies, retirement age, investment allocations, or retirement income sources as needed to align with evolving needs and objectives.

8. **Seek Professional Guidance:**

   - Consult with a financial advisor, retirement planner, or Certified Financial Planner (CFP) to develop a comprehensive retirement plan tailored to your specific goals, risk tolerance, and financial situation.

   - Professional advisors can provide personalized guidance, retirement savings projections, investment recommendations, and retirement income strategies based on your unique circumstances and objectives.

By carefully calculating retirement savings goals and developing a well-structured retirement plan, individuals can take proactive steps to ensure financial security, independence, and peace of mind in retirement. Start early, save consistently, and regularly review and adjust your retirement plan to stay on track towards achieving your retirement dreams.

- Strategies for maximizing retirement savings and minimizing taxes

Maximizing retirement savings and minimizing taxes are essential components of effective retirement planning. By implementing strategic savings strategies and tax-efficient investment techniques, individuals can optimize their retirement savings growth while minimizing tax liabilities. Here's a comprehensive discussion of strategies for maximizing retirement savings and minimizing taxes:

1. **Take Advantage of Employer-Sponsored Retirement Plans:**

   - Contribute to employer-sponsored retirement plans, such as 401(k), 403(b), or 457(b) plans, if available. These plans offer tax-deferred growth on contributions and may include employer-matching contributions, effectively doubling your savings.

   - Maximize contributions to employer-sponsored plans up to the annual contribution limits set by the Internal Revenue Service (IRS). For 2022, the contribution limit for 401(k) plans is $20,500, with an additional $6,500 catch-up contribution allowed for individuals aged 50 or older.

2. **Utilize Individual Retirement Accounts (IRAs):**

   - Contribute to traditional IRAs or Roth IRAs to supplement employer-sponsored retirement savings. Traditional IRA contributions may be tax deductible, providing immediate tax benefits, while

Roth IRA contributions are made with after-tax dollars but offer tax-free withdrawals in retirement.

- Maximize contributions to IRAs up to the annual limits set by the IRS. For 2022, the contribution limit for IRAs is $6,000, with an additional $1,000 catch-up contribution allowed for individuals aged 50 or older.

3. Consider Health Savings Accounts (HSAs):

- Contribute to Health Savings Accounts (HSAs) if enrolled in a high-deductible health plan (HDHP). HSAs offer triple tax benefits: contributions are tax-deductible, earnings grow tax-free, and withdrawals are tax-free when used for qualified medical expenses.

- Maximize contributions to HSAs up to the annual limits set by the IRS. For 2022, the contribution limit for HSAs is $3,650 for individuals with self-only coverage and $7,300 for individuals with family coverage, with an additional $1,000 catch-up contribution allowed for individuals aged 55 or older.

4. **Implement Roth Conversion Strategies:**

- Consider converting traditional retirement account assets, such as traditional IRAs or 401(k) plans, to Roth accounts. Roth conversions involve paying taxes on the converted amount upfront but allow for tax-free withdrawals in retirement, potentially reducing future tax liabilities.

- Evaluate the tax implications, including current and future tax rates, before executing Roth conversions. Timing conversions during low-income years or periods of lower tax rates can minimize tax impact.

5. **Employ Tax-Loss Harvesting and Capital Gains Management:**

- Implement tax-loss harvesting strategies in taxable investment accounts to offset capital gains and reduce tax liabilities. Tax-loss harvesting involves selling investments at a loss to realize capital losses, which can be used to offset capital gains and up to $3,000 of ordinary income per year.

- Manage capital gains by strategically timing asset sales to minimize tax consequences. Long-term capital gains, from investments held for more than one year, are taxed at lower rates than short-term capital gains, providing potential tax savings.

6. Optimize Asset Location:

- Place tax-efficient investments, such as stocks or stock index funds, in taxable brokerage accounts to take advantage of favorable capital gains tax rates. Tax-inefficient investments, such as bonds or actively managed funds generating high taxable income, are better suited for tax-deferred or tax-free accounts.

- Consider the tax implications of different investment types and account structures when allocating assets across taxable, tax-deferred, and tax-free accounts.

7. Plan for Required Minimum Distributions (RMDs):

- Be aware of required minimum distributions (RMDs) from traditional retirement accounts, such as traditional IRAs and 401(k) plans, starting at age 72 (previously age 70½). Failure to take RMDs can result in significant tax penalties.

- Strategically manage RMDs by coordinating withdrawals with other sources of retirement income and considering tax implications. Qualified charitable distributions (QCDs) allow individuals aged 70½ or older to donate up to $100,000 per year directly from their IRAs to charity, satisfying RMD requirements while reducing taxable income.

8. **Consult with Tax and Financial Professionals:**

- Seek guidance from tax advisors, financial planners, or Certified Public Accountants (CPAs) to develop personalized retirement savings and tax planning strategies. Professional advisors can provide insights, recommendations, and tax-efficient solutions tailored to your specific financial situation, goals, and objectives.

By implementing these strategies for maximizing retirement savings and minimizing taxes, individuals can enhance the growth of their retirement nest eggs, optimize tax efficiency, and achieve their long-term financial goals with greater confidence and security. Regular review and adjustment of retirement plans in response to changes in tax laws, personal circumstances, and financial goals are essential for staying on track towards a successful retirement.

CHAPTER 5: ADVANCED WEALTH CREATION STRATEGIES

Welcome to Chapter 5: Advanced Wealth Creation Strategies. In this chapter, we delve into the realm of sophisticated techniques and strategies designed to accelerate wealth accumulation, optimize investment returns, and achieve financial independence. Building upon the foundational principles of personal finance and investment management, advanced wealth creation strategies offer innovative approaches to grow assets, mitigate risks, and maximize long-term prosperity.

While basic financial concepts provide a solid framework for managing finances and building wealth, advanced strategies take financial planning to the next level, offering opportunities for enhanced wealth creation and preservation. Whether you're a seasoned investor seeking to refine your approach or an ambitious individual looking to accelerate wealth accumulation, this chapter will equip you with the knowledge, tools, and strategies needed to elevate your financial success.

Throughout this chapter, we'll explore a range of advanced wealth-creation strategies, including:

- Leveraging alternative investments such as real estate, private equity, hedge funds, and venture capital to diversify portfolios and generate higher returns.

- Implementing tax optimization techniques, such as tax-loss harvesting, capital gains deferral, and estate planning strategies, to minimize tax liabilities and preserve wealth.

- Utilizing advanced investment vehicles, including structured products, derivatives, and options strategies, to hedge risks, enhance returns, and capitalize on market opportunities.

- Incorporating advanced retirement planning techniques, such as Roth conversions, backdoor Roth IRAs, and mega backdoor Roth contributions, to maximize retirement savings and tax efficiency.

- Exploring advanced asset protection strategies, including offshore trusts, limited liability companies (LLCs), and irrevocable trusts, to safeguard assets from creditors and legal liabilities.

By mastering these advanced wealth-creation strategies, individuals can unlock new avenues for financial growth, security, and prosperity. However, it's important to approach these strategies with caution, diligence, and a thorough understanding of their risks, complexities, and potential rewards. Consulting with financial professionals, including certified financial planners, tax advisors, and investment experts, can provide invaluable guidance and ensure that advanced wealth creation strategies are aligned with your goals, risk tolerance, and financial circumstances.

Whether you aspire to achieve financial independence, leave a legacy for future generations, or pursue your passions and dreams without financial constraints, the advanced wealth creation strategies outlined in this chapter offer a roadmap to realize your aspirations and build a legacy of lasting prosperity. So, let's embark on this journey of exploration and discovery as we uncover the secrets to advanced wealth creation and financial empowerment.

- Diversification and asset allocation

Diversification and asset allocation are fundamental principles of investment management aimed at reducing risk and optimizing returns within an investment portfolio. By spreading investments across different asset classes, sectors, industries, and geographic regions, diversification helps minimize the impact of individual asset or market fluctuations on overall portfolio performance. Asset allocation, on the other hand, involves strategically distributing assets across various investment categories based on risk tolerance, investment goals, and time horizon. Here's a comprehensive discussion on diversification and asset allocation:

1. **Diversification:**

   - **Definition:** Diversification is the practice of spreading investment capital across a wide range of assets to reduce exposure to any single investment or risk factor. The goal of diversification is to minimize portfolio volatility and enhance risk-adjusted returns by mitigating the impact of individual asset performance on overall portfolio performance.

   - **Types of Diversification:**

     - **Asset Class Diversification:** Allocating investments across different asset classes, such as stocks, bonds, cash equivalents, real estate, commodities, and alternative investments, to achieve a balance of risk and return.

- **Sector and Industry Diversification:** Investing in companies across different sectors and industries to reduce concentration risk and exposure to sector-specific factors or market cycles.

- **Geographic Diversification:** Spreading investments across domestic and international markets to mitigate country-specific risks, currency fluctuations, geopolitical events, and economic conditions.

- **Company Size Diversification:** Investing in companies of varying market capitalizations, including large-cap, mid-cap, and small-cap stocks, to diversify exposure to company-specific risks and market dynamics.

- **Investment Style Diversification:** Allocating investments across different investment styles, such as growth, value, or blend strategies, to diversify factor exposures and capitalize on market opportunities.

- **Benefits of Diversification:**

  - **Risk Reduction:** Diversification helps reduce portfolio volatility and minimize the impact of adverse events or underperformance of individual assets on overall portfolio performance.

  - **Enhanced Risk-Adjusted Returns:** By spreading investments across multiple assets with different risk-return profiles, diversification can optimize risk-adjusted returns and improve the consistency of investment outcomes over time.

  - **Protection Against Market Volatility:** Diversification provides a buffer against market volatility, economic downturns, and unforeseen events, helping investors navigate turbulent market conditions with greater resilience.

  - **Increased Stability and Consistency:** A well-diversified portfolio is less susceptible to extreme fluctuations in value, providing investors with greater stability, predictability, and peace of mind, especially during periods of market uncertainty.

- **Potential for Long-Term Growth:**

Diversification allows investors to capture growth opportunities across different sectors, regions, and asset classes, fostering long-term wealth accumulation and financial success.

- **Considerations:**

- While diversification can reduce risk, it does not guarantee against losses or eliminate the possibility of investment underperformance.

- Over diversification, or spreading investments too thinly across too many assets, can dilute returns and hinder the ability to capitalize on high-conviction investment opportunities.

- Asset correlations may vary over time, especially during periods of market stress or systemic shocks, impacting the effectiveness of diversification strategies.

- Diversification does not replace the need for ongoing monitoring, review, and adjustment of investment portfolios to ensure alignment with changing financial goals, market conditions, and risk preferences.

2. **Asset Allocation:**

- **Definition:** Asset allocation is the strategic distribution of investment capital across different asset classes, such as stocks, bonds, and cash equivalents, based on an investor's risk tolerance, investment objectives, and time horizon. Asset allocation serves as the foundation of portfolio construction and plays a critical role in determining overall portfolio risk and return characteristics.

- **Components of Asset Allocation:**

  - **Strategic Asset Allocation:** Establishing target asset allocations based on long-term investment goals, risk tolerance, and return expectations. Strategic asset allocation sets the framework for portfolio construction and provides guidelines for ongoing investment decisions.

  - **Tactical Asset Allocation:** Making short-term adjustments to asset allocations based on market conditions, economic outlook, valuation metrics, or other factors impacting investment opportunities and risk profiles. Tactical asset allocation allows investors to capitalize on short-term market inefficiencies or mispricings.

- **Dynamic Asset Allocation:** Employing dynamic asset allocation strategies that adapt to changing market conditions, investor preferences, or life cycle stages. Dynamic asset allocation involves periodic reassessment and rebalancing of asset allocations to maintain alignment with evolving financial goals and risk preferences.

- **Benefits of Asset Allocation:**

- **Risk Management:** Asset allocation helps manage portfolio risk by diversifying investments across different asset classes with varying risk-return profiles. By spreading investments across multiple asset classes, asset allocation reduces the impact of adverse events or underperformance of individual assets on overall portfolio performance.

- **Return Optimization:** Asset allocation optimizes portfolio returns by balancing risk and return considerations and capitalizing on opportunities across different asset classes and market segments. Strategic asset allocation allows investors to capture growth potential while mitigating downside risk.

- **Customization and Flexibility:** Asset allocation provides investors with flexibility to tailor portfolios to their unique financial goals, risk tolerance, and investment preferences. By adjusting asset allocations based on changing market conditions or personal circumstances, investors can adapt their portfolios to evolving needs and objectives.

- **Long-Term Wealth Accumulation:** Asset allocation supports long-term wealth accumulation by fostering disciplined and systematic investment strategies that prioritize consistency, diversification, and risk management. By adhering to strategic asset allocation principles, investors can navigate market cycles and achieve sustainable wealth growth over time.

- **Considerations:**

  - Asset allocation should be based on individual factors such as risk tolerance, investment goals, time horizon, and financial circumstances. There is no one-size-fits-all approach to asset allocation, and allocations may vary significantly from one investor to another.

  - Regular monitoring and rebalancing of asset allocations are essential to maintain alignment with financial goals, risk tolerance, and market conditions. Rebalancing involves adjusting portfolio allocations periodically to restore target asset weights and minimize deviations from strategic targets.

  - Asset allocation decisions should consider factors such as market valuations, economic indicators, interest rates, inflation expectations, and geopolitical risks. By incorporating fundamental and technical analysis into asset allocation decisions, investors can make informed judgments about portfolio positioning and risk management.

In summary, diversification and asset allocation are cornerstones of effective investment management, providing investors with powerful tools to optimize risk-adjusted returns, manage portfolio volatility, and achieve long-term financial goals. By employing disciplined and systematic approaches to diversification and asset allocation, investors can build robust investment portfolios that withstand market fluctuations, capitalize on growth opportunities, and navigate the path to financial success with confidence and resilience.

- Tax-efficient investing

Tax-efficient investing is a strategy aimed at minimizing tax liabilities on investment income and maximizing after-tax returns within an investment portfolio. By strategically managing investment decisions, asset locations, and tax strategies, investors can optimize tax efficiency and enhance long-term wealth accumulation. Here's a comprehensive discussion on tax-efficient investing:

1. **Understanding Taxation of Investment Income:**

- **Types of Investment Income:** Investment income can be categorized into different types for tax purposes, including:

- **Ordinary Income:** Generated from interest income, dividends, and short-term capital gains, taxed at ordinary income tax rates.

- **Qualified Dividends and Long-Term Capital Gains:** Qualified dividends and long-term capital gains are subject to preferential tax rates, typically lower than ordinary income tax rates.

- **Tax-Exempt Income:** Certain investments, such as municipal bonds or tax-exempt mutual funds, generate tax-exempt income that is not subject to federal income taxes.

- **Tax Deferral:** Tax-deferred investment accounts, such as traditional IRAs, 401(k) plans, and annuities, allow investors to defer taxes on investment income until withdrawals are made in retirement. Tax-deferred growth can enhance investment returns over time by compounding investment gains without immediate tax consequences.

2. Implementing Tax-efficient Investment Strategies:

- **Asset Location:** Place tax-efficient investments, such as stocks with qualified dividends or tax-exempt municipal bonds, in taxable brokerage accounts to take advantage of preferential tax treatment. Tax-inefficient investments, such as bonds or actively managed funds generating high taxable income, are better suited for tax-deferred or tax-free accounts.

- **Tax-loss Harvesting:** Harvest capital losses in taxable investment accounts to offset capital gains and reduce tax liabilities. Tax-loss harvesting involves selling investments at a loss to realize capital losses, which can be used to offset capital gains and up to $3,000 of ordinary income per year. Excess losses can be carried forward to future tax years.

- **Capital Gains Management:** Manage capital gains by strategically timing asset sales to minimize tax consequences. Long-term capital gains, from investments held for more than one year, are taxed at lower rates than short-term capital gains, providing potential tax savings. Consider selling investments in years with lower income or capital gains tax rates.

- **Roth Conversions:** Convert assets from traditional retirement accounts, such as traditional IRAs or 401(k) plans, to Roth accounts to take advantage of tax-free withdrawals in retirement. Roth conversions involve paying taxes on the converted amount upfront but can provide tax-free growth and withdrawals, especially in retirement.

- **Qualified Charitable Distributions (QCDs):** Make charitable donations directly from traditional IRAs to qualified charities once you reach age 72 (previously age 70½) to satisfy required minimum distributions (RMDs) and reduce taxable income. Qualified charitable distributions (QCDs) allow individuals aged 72 or older to donate up to

$100,000 per year directly from their IRAs to charity, satisfying RMD requirements while reducing taxable income.

3. **Utilizing Tax-advantaged Accounts:**

- **Employer-sponsored Retirement Plans:** Contribute to tax-deferred employer-sponsored retirement plans, such as 401(k) plans or 403(b) plans, to defer taxes on contributions and investment gains until retirement. Employer matching contributions and catch-up contributions for individuals aged 50 or older can further enhance retirement savings.

- **Individual Retirement Accounts (IRAs):** Contribute to traditional IRAs or Roth IRAs to supplement employer-sponsored retirement savings. Traditional IRA contributions may be tax deductible, providing immediate tax benefits, while Roth IRA contributions offer tax-free withdrawals in retirement.

- **Health Savings Accounts (HSAs):** Contribute to HSAs if enrolled in a high-deductible health plan

(HDHP) to save for medical expenses tax-free. HSAs offer triple tax benefits: contributions are tax-deductible, earnings grow tax-free, and withdrawals are tax-free when used for qualified medical expenses.

4. **Considerations for Tax-efficient Investing:**

   - **Long-term Perspective:** Tax-efficient investing strategies are most effective when implemented with a long-term perspective, allowing for the compounding of tax-advantaged investment returns over time.

   - **Tax Law Changes:** Stay informed about changes in tax laws, regulations, and policies that may impact investment decisions and tax planning strategies. Tax laws are subject to change, and adjustments to tax-efficient strategies may be necessary in response to legislative or regulatory developments.

   - **Personalized Approach:** Tax-efficient investing strategies should be tailored to individual circumstances, financial goals, risk tolerance, and tax situations. There is no one-size-fits-all approach to tax planning, and strategies may vary based on factors such as income level, investment objectives, and retirement goals.

5. **Consultation with Financial Professionals:**

   - Consult with tax advisors, financial planners, or Certified Public Accountants (CPAs) to develop personalized tax-efficient investment strategies aligned with your specific financial situation, goals, and objectives. Professional advisors can provide insights, recommendations, and tax-efficient solutions tailored to your unique circumstances.

By incorporating tax-efficient investing strategies into your investment approach, you can optimize after-tax returns, minimize tax liabilities, and enhance long-term wealth accumulation. Tax-efficient investing allows you to keep more of your investment gains and achieve your financial goals with greater efficiency and effectiveness.

- Estate planning and wealth preservation techniques

Estate planning is a critical component of comprehensive financial management aimed at preserving and transferring wealth to future generations while minimizing estate taxes, probate costs, and administrative burdens. Effective estate planning involves a combination of legal, financial, and tax strategies tailored to an individual's unique circumstances, goals, and objectives. Here's a comprehensive discussion on estate planning and wealth preservation techniques:

1. **Understanding Estate Planning:**

   - **Definition:** Estate planning is the process of arranging for the management and distribution of an individual's assets during their lifetime and after death. Estate planning encompasses various legal documents, financial arrangements, and tax strategies designed to protect assets, provide for loved ones, and ensure the fulfilment of personal wishes and intentions.

- Key Components:

- Will: A legal document that outlines how an individual's assets will be distributed upon their death and appoints an executor to administer the estate. A will allows individuals to specify beneficiaries, designate guardians for minor children, and address other important matters related to estate distribution.

- Trusts: Legal arrangements that hold assets on behalf of beneficiaries, managed by a trustee according to specific terms and instructions outlined in the trust agreement. Trusts can serve various purposes, including asset protection, wealth transfer, tax planning, and charitable giving.

- Power of Attorney: Legal authorization granted to a designated individual (attorney-in-fact) to make financial or healthcare decisions on behalf of the grantor in the event of incapacity or disability.

- **Healthcare Directive (Living Will):** A legal document that specifies an individual's preferences for medical treatment and end-of-life care in case of incapacitation or terminal illness.

- **Beneficiary Designations:** Designate beneficiaries for retirement accounts, life insurance policies, and other financial assets to ensure proper distribution outside of probate and by the individual's wishes.

- **Objectives:**

- **Asset Protection:** Shield assets from creditors, lawsuits, and other legal claims through the use of trusts, limited liability entities, and other asset protection strategies.

- **Wealth Transfer:** Facilitate the transfer of assets to intended beneficiaries, such as family members, charities, or other heirs, while minimizing estate taxes, probate costs, and administrative expenses.

- **Tax Planning:** Implement tax-efficient strategies to minimize estate taxes, gift taxes, income taxes, and generation-skipping transfer taxes on transferred assets.

  - Family Harmony: Prevent disputes, conflicts, and misunderstandings among family members by clearly articulating intentions, expectations, and responsibilities regarding estate distribution and inheritance.

  - Charitable Giving: Support charitable causes and organizations through planned giving strategies, such as charitable trusts, donor-advised funds, and bequests in wills or trusts.

2. **Wealth Preservation Techniques:**

  - Lifetime Gifting: Transfer assets to beneficiaries during the grantor's lifetime through annual gift tax exclusions, lifetime gift tax exemptions, and other gifting strategies to reduce the size of the taxable estate and maximize tax-free transfers.

  - Irrevocable Trusts: Establish irrevocable trusts to remove assets from the taxable estate, protect assets from creditors, and facilitate wealth transfer to beneficiaries while retaining certain benefits and control over trust assets.

- **Life Insurance Planning:** Utilize life insurance policies as a wealth preservation tool to provide liquidity for estate taxes, fund buy-sell agreements, equalize inheritances among heirs, and create a legacy for future generations.

- **Family Limited Partnerships (FLPs) and Limited Liability Companies (LLCs):** Structure ownership of family assets through FLPs or LLCs to centralize management, protect assets from creditors, and facilitate tax-efficient wealth transfer through gifting or sales of partnership interests.

- **Charitable Trusts and Foundations:** Establish charitable remainder trusts (CRTs), charitable lead trusts (CLTs), or private foundations to support charitable causes, receive tax benefits, and preserve family wealth while leaving a lasting legacy.

- **Estate Freeze Techniques:** Implement estate freeze strategies, such as grantor retained annuity trusts (GRATs), intentionally defective grantor trusts (IDGTs), or sales to defective grantor trusts (IDGT sales), to lock in the value of appreciating assets and transfer future appreciation to beneficiaries tax-efficiently.

- **Asset Protection Strategies:** Protect assets from potential threats, including lawsuits, divorce, bankruptcy, and creditor claims, through the use of asset protection trusts, domestic asset protection structures, and other legal entities designed to safeguard wealth.

- **Business Succession Planning:** Plan for the orderly transition of family-owned businesses or closely held entities to the next generation, including leadership succession, ownership transfer, and tax-efficient exit strategies.

3. **Regular Review and Updates:**

 - Estate plans should be reviewed periodically and updated as needed to reflect changes in personal circumstances, family dynamics, tax laws, and financial goals. Life events such as marriage, divorce, the birth of children or grandchildren, changes in health, relocation, significant asset acquisitions or disposals, and legislative or regulatory changes may necessitate revisions to existing estate plans.

- Regular communication with legal advisors, financial planners, tax professionals, and other trusted advisors is essential to ensure that estate planning strategies remain current, effective, and aligned with evolving objectives.

4. **Professional Guidance and Collaboration:**

- Estate planning is a complex and specialized field that requires expertise in legal, financial, and tax matters. Collaborate with experienced professionals, including estate planning attorneys, financial advisors, tax specialists, and trust officers, to develop comprehensive estate plans tailored to your specific needs, goals, and objectives.

- Professional advisors can provide personalized guidance, strategic recommendations, and technical expertise to navigate the complexities of estate planning, minimize tax liabilities, and preserve wealth for future generations.

5. **Open Communication and Transparency:**

- Foster open communication and transparency among family members regarding estate planning intentions, objectives, and arrangements. Discussing estate planning matters openly can help prevent misunderstandings, alleviate concerns, and promote family harmony and unity.

In conclusion, estate planning and wealth preservation techniques are essential components of a comprehensive financial strategy aimed at protecting assets, providing for loved ones, and fulfilling personal wishes and intentions. By incorporating legal, financial, and tax strategies tailored to individual circumstances and objectives, individuals can effectively manage and transfer wealth across generations while minimizing taxes, maximizing benefits, and leaving a lasting legacy for future generations. Regular review, collaboration with professional advisors, and open communication among family members are key elements of successful estate planning and wealth preservation.

CONCLUSION

In conclusion, "Financial Fitness: Mastering Money Management and Wealth Creation" serves as a comprehensive guide to achieving financial well-being, security, and prosperity. Throughout this book, we've explored essential principles, strategies, and techniques for managing money effectively, building wealth, and securing a stable financial future.

From understanding the fundamentals of personal finance to mastering advanced wealth creation strategies, each chapter has provided valuable insights, practical advice, and actionable steps to empower readers on their financial journey. By embracing the principles of financial fitness and implementing sound money management practices, individuals can take control of their finances, overcome common challenges, and unlock new opportunities for financial success.

We've discussed the importance of setting clear financial goals, creating realistic budgets, and establishing emergency funds to weather unexpected expenses and life events. We've explored the significance of managing debt responsibly, investing wisely, and planning for retirement to build long-term wealth and achieve financial independence.

Furthermore, we've examined advanced strategies for maximizing investment returns, minimizing taxes, and preserving wealth for future generations through effective estate planning techniques. By incorporating tax-efficient investing strategies, asset protection measures, and wealth transfer mechanisms, individuals can optimize their financial resources, minimize risks, and leave a lasting legacy for their loved ones.

Financial fitness is not just about accumulating wealth; it's about achieving financial freedom, peace of mind, and fulfillment. It's about aligning your financial decisions with your values, priorities, and aspirations. It's about making informed choices today that will positively impact your future and the future of those you care about.

As you embark on your journey to financial fitness, remember that it's not a sprint but a marathon. It requires discipline, perseverance, and a commitment to lifelong learning and improvement. Stay focused on your goals, stay adaptable to changing circumstances, and seek guidance from trusted advisors along the way.

I hope that "Financial Fitness: Mastering Money Management and Wealth Creation" has provided you with the knowledge, tools, and inspiration to take control of your financial destiny and achieve the life of abundance and prosperity you deserve. May you embrace the principles of financial fitness with confidence, courage, and optimism as you navigate the exciting path ahead. Here's to your continued success and prosperity.

www.ingramcontent.com/pod-product-compliance
Lightning Source LLC
Chambersburg PA
CBHW070156230526
45471CB00002B/686